MW00974875

Love. Faith. Endurance.

By: Brandon "Breeze" Dawson

Dedication

I dedicate this book to Jesus Christ, my Lord, because without Him I am nothing.

I also dedicate this book to all those who have dreams in their hearts and feel like God has forgotten about them. God hasn't forgotten about you, He placed those dreams there for a reason, and I pray that as you read these pages you are equipped with the strength to pursue them wholeheartedly. God Loves you, and so do I.

- Brandon "Breeze" Dawson

Introduction

"The word of God steadies me. He says your trials and tribulations make you who you are. So, you can see my whole story in the way I endured and overcame some testing experiences."

Evander Holyfield

There is something to be learned from every trial that we go through. Often times as we go through our trials the only thing that we can think about is how to get out of them. Yet it's funny that the only time we see breakthrough is when we stop and think about what we can learn from the things we are currently going through.

Throughout the pages of this book, you'll find the poems I wrote to Jesus as I was going through some of my trials. In the midst of my trials, it felt as though He was a million miles away and had no interest in rescuing me from my distress; but the more I began to learn about Him, I realized that He was right there with me and He didn't plan on leaving anytime soon. I pray that as you embark on this 40-day devotional series, you'll come to the same realization.

The Gift of Rest (Day 1)

Jesus,

I've been traveling this path for a while now, and it seems like an endless quest,

It's a cycle of trial and tribulation, my patience is being put to the test.

I've come to the end of myself, realizing I don't know what's best,

I'm tired of carrying these burdens, so I come to You for my rest.

Matthew 11:28 NLT

Then Jesus said, *"come to me all of you who are weary and carry heavy burdens, and I will give you rest."*

God never designed us to carry burdens in our lives; instead we were created to operate out of a place of rest. God has already made plans to relieve us of the burdens that we do carry; and trust is the key that will open the door to those plans.

Our Provider (Day 2)

Lord,

Some situations seem bleak, like I'm swimming against the tide,

So I call on Jehovah-jireh, for I know He will provide.

My problems might seem big, but to You they're oh so small,

No needs for worry in this world, for You, have overcome it all.

If you can split the sea for the Israelites, and blow the wet ground dry,

Then there's nothing You can't do for me, Lord, You are The Most High.

Genesis 22:13-14 NLT

"Then Abraham looked up and saw a ram caught by its horns in a thicket. So he took the ram and sacrificed it as a burnt offering in place of his son. Abraham named that place Yahweh-Yireh (Jehovah-Jireh, which means "The Lord will provide"). To this day, people still use that name as a proverb: "On the mountain of The Lord it will be provided."

Sometimes we look at life's obstacles and forget just how big our God is; there will never be a situation that's too tough for Him to handle. He has promised to provide for us, and all He asks in return is our trust.

Restoration (Day 3)

Jesus,

I talked to a lady today, whose son recently died,

The cops say he shot himself, but she refuses to believe those lies.

Her blue eyes revealed the pain that was growing on the inside,

Her heart, up and down constantly, like a roller coaster ride.

She asked me if I thought her son would make it to Heaven,

And I told her, "Ma'am, I don't know the answer to that question."

"But what I do know is that God is in the business of restoration,

Only He can bring you peace and remove your confusion and frustration."

Job 42:10 NLT

When Job prayed for his friends, The Lord restored his fortunes. In fact, The Lord gave him twice as much as before.

Satan comes to kill, steal and destroy, but its God's will that we live abundant and prosperous lives. He wants to restore everything that has been taken from us.

Confidence (Day 4)

Jesus,

I will hold on to my belief that You will do all that You say You can,

And I will continue to trust You Lord, even when I don't fully understand.

The things that I've endured will not be in vain,

Yet every trial that I've overcome will bring glory to Your name.

Hebrews 10:35-36 NLT

So do not throw away this confident trust in The Lord. Remember the great reward it brings you! Patient endurance is what you need now, so that you will continue to do God's will. Then you will receive all that he has promised.

There is a great reward for those who remain confident in The Lord. If we continue to push through obstacles that may arise and never lose trust in Him, then we will receive everything that He has promised us.

God's Plan (Day 5)

Jesus,

You've given me these dreams,

Which are plans, not schemes,

And as impossible as they may seem,

Can only be achieved by Your means.

By faith I focus on these dreams,

And by faith You fulfill them,

And of course the enemy appears and does his absolute best to kill them.

Fear, distractions, failure, shame and doubt,

These are the tools Satan uses to rub my dreams out.

But I've stripped off those weights that pulled me to the ground,

And run this race with endurance, with no signs of slowing down.

"For I know the plans I have for you" says The Lord, 'they are good and not evil."

"To mount wings on your back, and watch you fly like an eagle."

Jeremiah 29:11 NLT

"For I know the plans I have for you" says The Lord. "They are plans for good and not for disaster, to give you a future and hope."

Regardless of the mistakes we've made, God has good plans for our lives. It's not a part of His plan for us to be insufficient in anything we do. His plan is for us to prosper in every area of life; spiritually, physically and financially.

The Power of Grace (Day 6)

Jesus,

Healing starts in the mind long before it begins in the vessel,

We receive it through faith, which is why Grace is so special.

Grace has done so much, and met all of our needs,

It's given us the things that can't be attained by our numerous degrees.

It gives us everything that pertains to Godliness and life,

It plants us in rest and removes stress and strife.

It has made us partakers, of your divine nature,

It has given us the very essence of our Lord and Savior.

To live a life that pleases God, we have everything we need,

You accomplished so much by getting on that cross to bleed.

2 Peter 1:3 NLT

By His divine power, God has given us everything we need for living a Godly life. We have received all of this by coming to know Him, the one who called us to himself by means of his marvelous glory and excellence.

God has given us everything we need to live a life that pleases Him. A life that pleases Him prospers in every area; spiritually, physically and financially. And the more we get to know Him, the more will be revealed to us on how to live a life that pleases Him.

The Love (Day 7)

Jesus,

Why do we hurt the people who Love us the most?

Why do we push away the ones who we want to keep close?

Maybe it's because we're deeply rooted in fear,

Our minds are filled with doubts that we've never taken time to clear.

We're hurt people so we choose to hurt others,

Including those closest to us; our mothers, fathers, sisters and brothers.

But Your Love creeps in and plants seeds in our hearts and minds,

The Love You give is patient and kind.

The Love You give is bold and courageous,

The Love You give is the Love that saves us.

1 Corinthians 13:4 NLT

Love is patient and kind. Love is not jealous or boastful or proud or rude. It does not demand its own way. It is not irritable, and it keeps no record of being wronged. It does not rejoice about injustice but rejoices whenever the truth wins out. Love never gives up, never loses faith, is always hopeful, and endures through every circumstance.

To truly Love someone means to treat them the way that you would want to be treated. It means to show them respect, patience and kindness. Never give up on those around you and encourage them on their journey.

Christ, My Strength (Day 8)

Jesus,

I can't do anything without You,

Not even the simplest of tasks, such as tying my shoes.

I stopped believing in me and started believing in You,

Because what I was trying to get done, was blocking out what You wanted to do.

All these good things in my life came from Your hands,

It had nothing to do with my labor or my half-executed plans.

Philippians 4:13 KJV

I can do all things through Christ which strengtheneth me.

In ourselves we are limited in the things that we can achieve, but through Christ there's nothing we can't do. By trusting Him completely in every situation, He makes all things possible for us.

Trust (Day 9)

Jesus,

Trust can be a tough word to define,

Mom told us she had a tumor in her brain, but she would be fine.

I didn't really know how to feel at the time,

I was a young boy, around the age of 9.

Every time I thought about it, I would cry,

"Please Lord, don't let my mother die."

Time went on and things seemed alright,

My mom is strong, she was born to fight.

She put her faith and trust in Your hands,

Knowing soon You would reveal Your plans.

I was 23, one Friday evening,

My mom was still strong, and still believing.

She came to me with news about her head,

The tumor was gone, that thing was dead.

That day Lord, I witnessed Your power,

You will always come through, no matter the time nor the hour.

Psalms 9:10 NLT

Those who know your name trust in you, for you, O Lord, do not abandon those who search for you.

The only thing The Lord asks of us is our complete trust. He wants us to trust Him in every area. The more we begin to trust Him with, the more He will be able to do in our lives.

Patience (Day 10)

Jesus,

I learned the definition of patience last night,

How it's consistent, unwavering and rejoices in Loves delight.

How it finds those who seek it,

And how its sister, wisdom, awards those who need it.

I learned patience from You, for You are the definition of it,

Regardless of my mistakes, You still call me Your beloved.

Patience is not just waiting around, but more like plotting a course,

A course that is achievable with You as our source.

Romans 15:5 NLT

May God, who gives this patience and encouragement, help you live in complete harmony with each other, as is fitting for followers of Jesus Christ.

To be patient means to be consistent in what you believe regardless of difficulty or opposition. In essence, patience is prolonged faith. What you believe for could take a while to manifest but remain steadfast knowing that God's timing is perfect and that He is developing you so you can handle everything He has for you.

God Cares for Me (Day 11)

Jesus,

Sometimes we get patience confused with fear,

Sometimes the desires of our heart get discouraged by the things we hear.

Sometimes we see our circumstances instead of keeping our eyes on You,

And sometimes we listen to the lies of the enemy instead of believing what's true.

We don't go after what's rightfully ours because of the fear of falling short,

So we sit back and make excuses for the dreams we often abort.

See, we wait for your instructions, but You've already told us what to do,

"Cast your cares upon me, for I truly care for you."

1 Peter 5:7 NLT

Give all your worries and cares to God, for He cares about you.

It's not our job to worry about how things will get done. It's our job to trust God and do all that He has instructed us to do, even if we don't see how it will benefit us. Worry and anxiety ultimately slow down the plan that God has for us instead of speeding it up. It's time for us to do our part, and rest so God can do His.

Love and Honor (Day 12)

Jesus,

My pride is shattered,

Torn and tattered,

Beaten and battered,

And I don't know which way to go regarding these earthly matters.

It seems as though hurt is a reoccurring pattern,

Circling me, like the rings of Saturn.

But in a small corner of my heart I feel Your Love,

Constantly pushing me to rise above.

The feeling is faint but it's stronger than my pride,

Your Love is always looking to change us, starting from the inside.

Proverbs 29:23 KJV

A man's pride shall bring him low: but honour shall uphold the humble in spirit.

Love and pride cannot exist in the same place. Jesus came and exemplified what true Love is, even during the last moments of his life. While on the cross He remained humble and asked His father to forgive the people that crucified Him. For Him to put the needs of the people who caused Him so much pain above His own was extremely honorable and showed Love in the purest form. He's still doing the same thing today. Even when we go against God's word, He's right there at the throne pleading our case to The Father, because He truly Loves us.

Steps (Day 13)

Jesus,

Thank You for waking me up to see the light of another day,

Thank You for being with me every step of the way.

Lord, speak through my vocal chords and think through my mind,

I abide in You, so all is fine.

But if trouble happens to come my way,

Thanks for Your wisdom, for I know what to do and say.

Direct my steps, so my feet do not slip,

Hold on to me today, with Your forever tight grip.

Psalms 37:23 NLT

The Lord directs the steps of the godly. He delights in every detail of their lives.

Contrary to popular belief, it's not God's will to take us on the most difficult path. He wants to guide our steps and be involved in every aspect of our lives. When we wait and listen for His instructions, He can bring us into the places He has destined for us without confusion.

Serenity (Day 14)

Jesus,

The trees are swaying in the wind,

And I feel a warm breeze on my skin.

The sunlight hits my face and I smile,

I haven't felt this good in a while.

I fall back, and let the sweet smell of Bermuda grass alleviate my stress,

Simple thoughts reveal your intricate plans for my success.

The sky is full of peace, and the clouds have a nice flow,

They move like they're dancing, as if they're putting on a show.

As a ladybug lands on my nose,

A great revelation is exposed.

"The trials you've endured have become your deposition,

I never intended for you to hurt, but to place you in a powerful position."

Your Love creeps over my life, like the sun over the horizon,

It's consistent and secure, the only Love I can abide in.

Isaiah 55:12 KJV

For ye shall go out with joy, and be led forth with peace: the mountains and the hills shall break forth before you into singing, and all the trees of the field shall clap their hands.

In this world, we're going to have trouble, but it's not God's will for us to remain there. Even in the midst of hard times God wants us to be filled with joy and guided by peace. That's His will for our lives.

Open Ears (Day 15)

Jesus,

Sometimes it's hard to hear You,

I run to a voice, but I don't come near You.

I open my eyes, only to realize,

It's the enemy, feeding me lies.

He's trying to steal my peace; he wants me to relinquish my joy.

You told me he came to steal, kill and destroy.

So I put Your word in my mouth, and abide in Your house.

You've sealed my spirit with Yours, so the evil can't get in, and the good can't get out.

I trust You, and erase my doubt.

See no fear can dwell here, because Your love is perfect,

Endured a few trials, but it's all been worth it.

With my ears and heart open, I have made the choice,

 To block out the enemy, and only obey Your voice.

John 10:27-28 NLT

My sheep hear my voice and I know them, and they follow me. I give them eternal life and they will never perish, and no one will snatch them out of my hand.

The Lord is our shepherd, and we are His sheep. As our shepherd, it's God's job to protect us, but He can only protect us if we listen for Him and obey His instructions. Lots of the time we don't understand why he is asking us to do a certain thing, but that's where trust comes into play. We must be confident that God is always going to put us in a position to grow and be successful.

Reconciliation (Day 16)

Jesus,

I'm sorry…

Sorry for the games I've played.

Sorry for the mistakes I've made.

Sorry for the times I've left when You've asked me to stay.

And I'm sorry for everyday I chose not to pray.

I see Your Love is where it's at,

So to the world I can never go back.

I'm running to You and I'm here to stay,

Regardless of what anyone might say.

See all I want is Love, that's what we all want in truth.

For so long we've searched for the wrong things, ultimately wasting our youth.

The tears are falling as I'm writing this, for all the time I've wasted,

I can't thank You enough, for viewing my life as sacred.

Colossians 3:13 NLT

Make allowance for each other's faults and forgive anyone who offends you. Remember, The Lord forgave you, so you must forgive others.

Many times we've gone against God's word just to fulfill our own selfish desires. Fortunately, we serve a forgiving God; a God who lifts us up and presents us as blameless before Him (Jude 1:24). When we ask Him for forgiveness and repent, He chooses not to remember our sins. Therefore, since He has forgiven us, we should forgive those who have offended us.

I See You (Day 17)

Jesus,

I see You in the lakes, rivers, forests and streams,

I see You in the creativity of my most amazing dreams.

I see You in the big things and the small,

I see You in the simplicity and complexity of it all.

When I'm alone, I can sense You near me,

And when I pray, I know You hear me.

You listen intently, providing me with all my needs,

And You're so gracious, forever shaping me into who You want me to be.

Your omnipresence is amazing, like nothing I've seen before,

There's no doubt in my mind, exactly who You're fighting for.

Jeremiah 29:12-13 NLT

In those days when you pray, I will listen. If you look for me wholeheartedly, you will find me.

God is always with us and He's always listening to our prayers. And if we begin to earnestly seek Him by prayer studying His word, He'll reveal himself to us in ways that we couldn't imagine.

Protecting Our Peace (Day 18)

Jesus,

There is nothing they can do to hurt me, because I've taken myself out the center,

Becoming offended might seem natural, but its intent is to always hinder.

Offense keeps us stuck in the past, therefore we're cheating on our future,

By choosing to be offended, we relinquish our peace to our accusers.

Psalms 119:165 KJV

Great peace have they which love thy law: and nothing shall offend them.

When we delight in God's law we choose not to be offended and ultimately remain in peace. Above all, peace is one of the most important things we can possess. We must protect it all costs.

Finishing the Race (19)

Lord,

I feel the enemy watching, waiting on me to slip,

I run the race with endurance, but in the end he causes me to trip.

2 feet from the finish, and I feel it all slipping away,

Broken and fatigued, I open my mouth to pray.

"Lord please help me, it feels like I'm under attack,

I've fallen and can't arise; the enemy is literally standing on my back."

But you replied with truth, like any good father would do,

Your words have such power, which causes endurance to ensue.

"Arise my child, and finish this race,

The enemy isn't strong enough to keep you from My grace.

You give him too much credit, he's not as strong as he seems,

He could never stop you, not even in his wildest dreams."

Romans 16:20 NLT

The God of peace will soon crush Satan under your feet. May the grace of our Lord Jesus be with you.

When we became a part of God's family, we were given certain authorities. One of which is authority over our enemy, Satan. For so long we've given him so much credit and made him seem stronger than what he is. In all actuality, he's been place beneath our feet. We can walk boldly every day knowing that he is defeated and has no power over us.

Growth (Day 20)

Jesus,

We're thankful just to know You and for how You've led us to grow,

We're reaching for the future now and letting things of the past go.

We read Your word daily and apply it to our lives,

And with application of this knowledge, we will soar clear skies.

Colossians 2:6-7 NLT

And now, just as you have accepted Christ Jesus as your Lord, you must continue to follow him. Let your roots grow down into him, and let your lives be built on him. Then your faith will grow strong in the truth you were taught, and you will overflow with thankfulness.

It's not God's will that we remain stagnant. He wants to see us grow in every area, and the key to that is growing in our knowledge of Him. The more we learn about Him and what He's done for us, the more thankful we will become, which will in turn propel us toward the will of God for our lives.

Regardless (Day 21)

Jesus,

Help me to always make the right decisions, no matter how hard it might be,

Help me to always treat people with Love and respect, regardless of how they treat me.

Since Your spirit is within me, I wanna walk, talk and act like You,

I wanna follow Your example, regardless of what the world might do.

Regardless of the situation, always show Love,

Keep my mind off the world and focus on the things above.

I know things can get hard and I might not know what to do,

But keep me around people who will always point me to You.

Regardless of how I feel, keep my mind sharp,

With Your word as my shield, I will always guard my heart.

Romans 12:2 NKJV

And do not be conformed to this world, but be transformed by the renewing of your mind, that you may prove what is that good and acceptable and perfect will of God.

In order to become all that God wants us to be we can't afford to have the same mindset as the world. We have to constantly renew our minds with the word of God so we can be equipped to handle any situation that may arise.

God's Imagination (Day 22)

Lord,

I'm in this airplane, way above the clouds,

And I can feel Your glorious presence reigning down.

I see mountains, trees and miles of flat lands,

And to think You created it all with your vast, righteous hands.

Your mind is so detailed, and imagination so vivid,

I can't even begin to fathom the amazing thoughts that dwell within it.

1 Corinthians 2:9 -10 NLT

That is what the scriptures mean when they say, "No eye has seen, no ear has heard, and no mind has imagined what God has prepared for those who Love him." But it was to us that God revealed these things by his Spirit. For his spirit searches out everything and shows us God's deep secrets.

As believers, God has given His spirit to dwell within us. His spirit is our helper, comforter and our guide. By His spirit, he also reveals to us His secrets and we receive spiritual truths. A true gift of Love that is.

I Make the Choice (Day 23)

Jesus,

Today, I will enjoy my freedom from the top of my head to the soles of my feet,

And I make the choice to let go of my emptiness and be full and complete.

I make the choice to smile, not only in my face, but to smile with my heart,

And not to let anger, bitterness or my fears tear my relationships apart.

I make the choice to not be offended by the things people do or say,

And I make the choice to enjoy this absolutely glorious day.

Proverbs 16:32 NKJV

He who is slow to anger is better than the mighty, and he who rules his spirit than he who takes a city.

Every day we have to make the right choice where our emotions are concerned. God has given us authority over all things (Psalms 8:6), which includes authority over our emotions. We all have emotions, but our emotions shouldn't control and determine the direction of our lives. The most powerful people on the planet are those who have control over their emotions.

A Helping Hand (Day 24)

Jesus,

Why is it considered being "weak" to ask for help?

Why do we look to carry these burdens all by ourselves?

We think we're demonstrating strength by rejecting the help of You and others,

But honestly, we're letting pride drag us even deeper into the gutter.

On top of that, we can't hear from You because our lives are full of clutter,

And if we can't listen to You, we definitely won't hear from one another.

See we're capable, and talented, all of this is factual,

But amazing things happen, when we allow You to put your "super" on our "natural."

Hebrews 13:5-6 NKJV

Let your conduct be without covetousness; be content with such things as you have. For he himself has said, "I will never leave you nor forsake you." So we may boldly say: "The Lord is my helper; I will not fear. What can man do to me?"

Jesus is the one that will never leave us under any circumstance and will be with us all the days of our lives. He's our helper and we can remain confident knowing that He'll help us; all we have to do is ask for His help. His help comes in various forms though and often times He'll send people to our aid. Let's step out of pride and not be so quick to reject the help of others, because we could very well be rejecting the help of The Lord.

Slow Progress (Day 25)

Jesus,

Why is it that we always expect the worst?

Why is it that we rarely seek You first?

Why have we been deceived into thinking we are to constantly struggle?

Why don't we believe that You're working for us, even if it's sometimes slow and subtle?

We are to expect good things, but we must know they take time,

Sometimes You do quick work, and other times it's a slow grind.

But we must remain thankful, because the blessing is not in the destination, We learn of You in the details of our journey, and with trust comes the manifestation.

Lamentations 3:25 NLT

The Lord is good to those who depend on Him, to those who search for Him.

To depend on The Lord means to fully trust Him and that can be tough when it seems like no progress is being made. But keep the faith and become more diligent in the search. God is always there and He's always working on our behalf. Everything isn't going to happen overnight; slow progress is always better that no progress.

Victory (Day 26)

Jesus,

I wanna be as bold as a lion,

I wanna make bold declarations from atop Mt. Zion.

I wanna face every situation without an ounce of doubt,

I wanna thank You in advance with a victorious shout.

 Because this battle is already won, we're fighting from victory, not for it,

And for all that was taken from us, we trust in You to restore it.

Proverbs 28:1 NLT

The wicked run away when no one is chasing them, but the righteous are bold as a lion.

God doesn't want us to be afraid. He didn't give us the spirit of fear; therefore, He wants us to stand up boldly knowing that we have overcome every situation that we may face and we are victorious.

Big Dreams (Day 27)

Jesus,

I have dreams of being free,

I have dreams of breaking limitations and doing what's best for me.

I have dreams of waking up to this life with a smile,

I have dreams of being victorious, regardless of the circumstance or trial.

I have dreams of walking over everything that has hindered my progress,

I have dreams of remaining steadfast no matter how difficult the process.

I dream of prosperous lives for myself and all those around me,

I dream of stepping boldly in faith because Your angels do surround me.

I dream of never being tired, but remaining at rest,

I dream of me with my arms wide prepared to receive Your best.

I even have dreams of leading people to You,

These dreams can be real, Lord, just show me what to do.

Acts 2:17 NLT

In the last days, God says, I will pour out my spirit upon all people. Your sons and daughters will prophesy. Your young men will see visions, and your old men will dream dreams.

Every dream that we have for our lives doesn't just have to be a dream. No matter how difficult it may seem remember this; God wouldn't have given you the dream if it couldn't be attained. Go for it.

Warfare (Day 28)

Jesus,

The battle isn't fought in the physical,

The war rages in our minds,

We've been trying to fight with our hands, and ultimately wasting time.

The enemy attacks our thinking, which causes us not to trust You,

Therefore putting restrictions on us, and limiting what You can do.

But defeat is a thing of the past, because through You we can do all things,

In Revelations 1:6 you ordained us as Priests and Kings.

Therefore the victory is ours, we are forever winning,

I'm following Your example and calling the end from the beginning.

Ephesians 6:12 NLT

For we are not fighting against flesh-and-blood enemies, but against evil rulers and authorities of the unseen world, against mighty powers in this dark world, and against evil spirits in the heavenly places

Our minds are the battle ground, and there will be a war raging every day and the decisions we make will determine who we authorize to operate in our lives; either God or Satan. Therefore, we shouldn't waste our time fighting against other people, instead we should be arming ourselves with The Word of God so we can fight the good fight of faith.

The Power of the Tongue (Day 29)

Jesus,

Life and death is in the power of the tongue, but this You already knew,

I think you demonstrated this best, after I read about the things You do.

You controlled the weather with Your words, by saying, "peace be still",

You cleanse the leapers and the sick, by simply saying, "be healed."

Yet we have the same authority, it's in the words we speak,

We have authority over this Earth, for You've given it to the meek.

Proverbs 18:20-21 NLT

Wise words satisfy like a good meal; the right words bring satisfaction. The tongue can bring death or life; those who love to talk will reap the consequences.

The direction of our lives will be determined by the words we speak. What we allow in our minds will eventually get to our hearts and what's in our hearts will eventually come out of our mouths. We have to make it a priority to only expose ourselves to things that will edify us spirit, soul and body.

The Storm (Day 30)

Jesus,

There's a storm raging on the inside,

Harsh winds, heavy rains, fierce lightning, and immense rip tides.

I feel like I'm alone in the boat,

At times I'm barely staying afloat.

With holes in my vessel, and my boat sinking fast,

I feel everything around me coming to a crash.

As I let it all go and fall beneath the waves,

I'm hoping to find rest in this watery grave.

I'm hoping to find satisfaction from all the worldly things I crave,

And I'm hoping to find happiness, and all-around better days.

As I'm floating to the bottom, I'm pulled to the top,

And when I reach the surface, I see the storm has stopped.

My boat has been repaired and I'm all around better,

I can sail smooth now and enjoy calmer weather.

Mark 4:39-40 NKJV

Then he arose and rebuked the wind, and said to the sea, "Peace, be still!" And the wind ceased and there was a great calm. But he said to them, "Why are you so fearful? How is it that you have no faith?"

Our power is in the words we speak, and we have authority over the storms in our lives just as Jesus did. When we go through a storm, that's not the time for us to be silent; that's when we are to find out what God's word says about the situation and speak to that very situation.

Peace (Day 31)

Jesus,

Your peace is a tool that uplifts the mind,

Your peace is a tool that transcends time.

With Your peace as our guide, our path is made clear,

Each step made in faith, unaffected by fear.

Your peace is hard to understand and even harder to explain,

But I'll continue to thank You and praise Your holy name.

Philippians 4:7 NLT

Then you will experience Gods peace, which exceeds anything we can understand. His peace will guard your hearts and minds as you live in Christ Jesus.

One of the greatest gifts we can possess is that of peace, and to be at peace means to be complete; nothing missing, and nothing broken. God's peace is what keeps us calm in the midst of a storm and helps us find our way when it seems like there is nowhere to go.

Unbroken Promises (Day 32)

Lord,

Your word is your bond; therefore it cannot be broken,

So, it will all come to pass, every word that You've spoken.

Your word cannot be changed, not even the slightest bit,

So, Your promises will be fulfilled, every word that has come off Your lips.

Psalms 89:34 NLT

No, I will not break my covenant; I will not take back a single word I have said.

God has made so many promises to us; promises that he will never break. The key to seeing these promises manifest is to actually spend time in His word and learn what His promises are. From there, it's only a matter of believing they can and will come to pass in our lives.

God's Gift (Day 33)

Jesus,

I can't explain where my mind goes when my pen meets the paper,

Feels like I've been freed, there's no feeling greater.

There's no feeling greater, than giving your life to The Savior,

Might as well do it now, there are no promises for later.

The words I put together are my form of worship,

I give You all the praise, because You're more than worth it.

See Your Grace is a gift, one we didn't deserve,

You made all the lines straight, even when we drew curves.

Ephesians 2:8-9 NKJV

For by grace you have been saved through faith, and that not of yourselves; it is the gift of God, not of works, lest anyone should boast.

By grace we have been saved and we now sit in heavenly places with Christ. God's grace is unearned favor; A gift that we didn't do anything to earn. And since we didn't do anything to earn it, we can't brag about it. We can only thank him for it. God isn't good to us because we're good; He's good to us because He's good.

Pride (Day 34)

Jesus,

I've seen pride cause great men to fall,

I've seen pride cause relationships to stall.

I've seen pride bring pain to the people we care most about,

And I've seen pride fill hearts with fear and doubt.

Not to mention pride is one of the 7 things our Heavenly father hates,

And if pride is in our hearts, we'll be hindered by its weight.

Pride is an inwardly directed emotion that focuses on ones self,

So by keeping our focus on us, it's impossible to help someone else.

But our focus is on You, and all the good things of Your Kingdom,

Therefore we put our pride aside, and we receive our freedom.

Proverbs 16:18 NLT

Pride goes before destruction, and haughtiness before a fall. Better to live humbly with the poor than to share plunder with the proud.

Pride is one of the things God hates. Reason for this is because pride separates us from Him and leads us to believe that we don't need Him. This keeps us in bondage to self-effort, and if we are in bondage to self-effort or self-righteousness, grace has no effect in our lives. Remaining humble allows us to receive God's instruction clearly.

The Shame (Day 35)

Jesus,

Shame is real, and it's robbed us all in the same manner,

It's kept us tied to our past, and let our errors become our banner.

It puts us in a state of paranoia where we always try to cover our mistakes,

Therefore, we can't be real, and are forced to live a life completely fake.

By being tied to our past, shame sabotages our future,

The cuts run so deep; they're far beyond the repair of any suture.

Now our hope is extinguished, and we're blinded from taking the next step,

So, pride and shame work together to drown us at greater depths.

But You did something greater; You carried shame for all of us,

Shame can no longer remain, when in Your name and works we trust.

Hebrews 8:12 NLT

And I will forgive their wickedness, and I will never again remember their sins.

The enemy will always look to bring shame in our lives. He will remind us of our past mistakes and try to tell us that we're not good enough to be used by God. Fortunately for us, God has promised us that He has chosen not to remember our sins and past mistakes. Therefore, we shouldn't either. Instead, we should press forward to the will of God for our lives. He has good things planned for each and every one of us.

Weaknesses (Day 36)

Jesus,

I'm weak, I'm weak!

And this task is far too much for me!

To abolish my fear and spread Your word,

What do You see in me?

To pluck me from the crowd and decree me as a leader,

Someone like me, who was a liar and a cheater.

I hated being weak, but now I embrace it every time,

Through all my weaknesses, that enables You to shine.

See the glory is for You, it's never been mine,

I thought my sin was too much, but Your Grace abounded every time.

2 Corinthians 12:9 AMP

But he said to me, "My grace is sufficient for you (My lovingkindness and My mercy are more than enough— always available—regardless of the situation); for (My) power is being perfected (and is completed and shows itself most effectively) in (your) weakness." Therefore, I will all the more gladly boast in my weaknesses, so that the power of Christ (may completely enfold me and) may dwell in me.

All of the good things in our lives come from God, not our own hands. So we have nothing to brag about, unless we are bragging about how good God is. Without His power flowing through us, we'd get nothing done. On our own, we are weak; but through Christ we are strong.

I Surrender (Day 37)

Jesus,

I surrender, I can't control my life, and my efforts don't seem to be working,

I'm working too hard to hold it down, and I constantly find myself hurting.

I'm just so accustomed to being in control, and making my own plans,

But today, I quit striving and put it all in Your hands.

As I stand on the shore, feet planted in the sand,

The enemy says it can't be done,

But through You I know it can.

So, I give You my life, with the sole promise to do Your will,

Knowing the amazing things You have for me, will no longer be concealed.

Luke 9:23 NKJV

Then he said to them all, "If anyone desires to come after me, let him deny himself, and take up his cross daily, and follow me. For whoever desires to save his life will lose it, but whoever loses his life for my sake will save it.

In order to be a follower of Christ, we have to carry our cross daily. Meaning, we have to set aside our selfish interest and be willing to endure whatever type of persecution comes our way for being a Christian. Only when we die to ourselves will we truly begin to live.

Everyday Temptations (Day 38)

Jesus,

It's thick, and I have to face it every day,

Everyday I'm tempted, the enemy begging me to stray.

"Come back to your old life, following Christ is much too hard,

I can get you what you want – money, clothes, women and cars."

But the things he promises will pass away with this world,

His schemes are not secure, yet easily unfurled.

But Jesus, the things You promise, will last me longer than a car or a Rolex,

For the things You promise will manifest in this life and the next.

James 1:13-15 NKJV

Let no one say when he is tempted, "I am tempted by God"; for God cannot be tempted by evil, nor does he himself tempt anyone. But each one is tempted when he is drawn away by his own desires and enticed. Then, when desire has conceived, it gives birth to sin; and sin, when it is full-grown, brings forth death.

God is not tempting us to teach us. There is no sin in Him; therefore, He can't tempt us to sin. God teaches us through His word, and we're tempted when we allow our selfish desires to control us instead of His word.

Authority over the Enemy
(Day 39)

Jesus,

You have given me power, so on this day I will not fall,

I have authority over lions, cobras, scorpions and all.

I tread upon the enemy, and trample him with my feet,

And with the power you've given, I will not taste defeat.

Luke 10:19 NKJV

Behold, I give unto you authority to trample on serpents and scorpions, and over all the power of the enemy, and nothing shall by any means hurt you.

Through Christ we have become more than conquerors and the victory is always with us, no matter what stands in our way. God has given us authority over the enemy; therefore, we can be bold knowing that there is nothing that he can do to stop us.

Until I Take My Last Breath (Day 40)

Jesus,

My legs are beyond tired, and they tremble with every step,

But I've vowed to keep pushing, until I take my last breath.

The obstacles are many, but I know that I'm blessed

So, I will not stop Lord, until I take my last breath.

As I transition through my days, the enemy speaks of my death,

But I'll condemn his false decrees, until I take my last breath.

2 Corinthians 10:4 NLT

We use God's mighty weapons, not worldly weapons, to knock down strongholds of human reasoning and destroy false arguments.

God's weapons are His word; we have been equipped with His word so we can break free from the limits of human reasoning and destroy the camps of the enemy. God has created us to be more than conquerors and has given us the weapons to do it. The more time we spend learning about His word, the more skilled we become with our weapons.

About The Author

Brandon Dawson is a native to Atlanta, Ga and grew up on the east side of the city in Stone Mountain and Decatur. He was raised in the church but formed a relationship with God in 2013 at the age of 21 after reading Mark Cahill's book entitled "Paradise." After graduating from Kennesaw State University in 2015, Brandon went on to play professional basketball overseas until the latter end of 2016. He and his wife, Nikki, married in 2017 and live in Atlanta.

"Love. Faith. Endurance." stems from Brandon's passion to help others overcome the obstacles that are preventing them from being what God has called them to be. "We all have a purpose, and it's not just going to happen. We have to trust God and fight for that purpose."

– Brandon "Breeze" Dawson

Made in the USA
Columbia, SC
20 July 2019